Casper's done some pretty exciting things:

- He's been to the moon with the Apollo 16 Astronauts, who named their command module after him!

- He's working for the United Nations Children's Emergency Fund (UNICEF) to help swell the fund used for needy children around the world!

- He's joined the Boy Scouts of America, to welcome new Cub Scouts into the fold!

- He's been in the movies in many languages!

- He's in eight different comic magazines, read by over 36 million Americans each year—and by many more all over the world in many languages.

- He's on over 400 different items—clothes, food, toys, games!

- *And now—Casper's in paperback books—this is the very first time!*

# Casper

## The Friendly Ghost

# Ghost

## Stories

**tempo books**

GROSSET & DUNLAP
A National General Company
Publishers    New York

HEE HEE... AT LAST I HAVE *MY* OWN *GHOST* FOR MY EXPERIMENTS!

I'M WORKING ON A NEW ANTI-GHOST POTION MADE WITH BIRDS' TAIL FEATHERS!

WHY DO YOU *HATE* GHOSTS?

I DON'T! I JUST HAPPEN TO BE IN THE *ANTI-GHOST BUSINESS!*

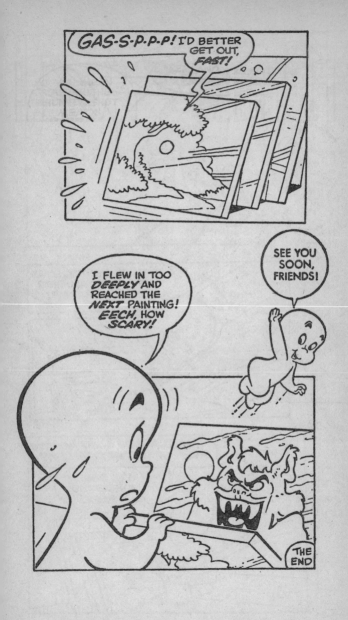